WRITERS REPUBLIC

A Closer Walk

Devotional
for Women

TEMPESST WALKER

Copyright © 2021 by Tempesst Walker.

All rights reserved. No part of this book may be reproduced in any form or by any electronic or mechanical means, including information storage and retrieval systems, without permission in writing from the publisher, except by reviewers, who may quote brief passages in a review.

This publication contains the opinions and ideas of its author. It is intended to provide helpful and informative material on the subjects addressed in the publication. The author and publisher specifically disclaim all responsibility for any liability, loss, or risk, personal or otherwise, which is incurred as a consequence, directly or indirectly, of the use and application of any of the contents of this book.

WRITERS REPUBLIC L.L.C.
515 Summit Ave. Unit R1
Union City, NJ 07087, USA

Website: *www.writersrepublic.com*
Hotline: *1-877-656-6838*
Email: *info@writersrepublic.com*

Ordering Information:
Quantity sales. Special discounts are available on quantity purchases by corporations, associations, and others. For details, contact the publisher at the address above.

Library of Congress Control Number: 2021933982
ISBN-13:   978-1-64620-625-4   [Paperback Edition]
                  978-1-64620-626-1   [Digital Edition]

Rev. date: 03/04/2021

I would like to thank my father God for keeping me and giving me the ability and gift to encourage all. It brings me so much joy. To my daughter Sahari Walker for giving me purpose to fight through every adversity and always telling me how strong, beautiful and what a wonderful mom I am to her. To you my family, friends and each of you that purchase my book I appreciate you.

Introduction

Hi, my name is Tempesst Walker. I am thirty-four years old. I love God and I love to encourage people from all walks of life It is my desire and purpose to inspire and encourages others even when life hands me some tough cards. A wise man former pastor Tyrone Smith of the Next Generation of The Original Morning Star Baptist church once told me life it is like playing cards you are dealt five in a difference and you just got to play your cards until you go out and win. I have learned that no matter how you shuffle the cards, or what kind of hand you are dealt you will win with Jesus.

Koby had a basketball…
David had a rock…
Moses had a rod…
My hand.
I was born 1986, a premature 1 pound and 14 ounces.
In 1991, my father died at the age of thirty-three from lymphoma cancer (I was five years old).
In 1999, I lost my little brother in a tragic event, uncle was shot and killed
In 2006, I lost everything due to Hurricane Katrina
In 2008, Grandmother died of a heart attack totally unexpectedly and gave birth to a beautiful little girl who's my everything: Sahari D' Unique Walker. They say when someone leaves this world it means a new birth is becoming …

In 2015, my ex-boyfriend got shot and was left blind and paralyzed. I stayed the course.
In 2017 I lost my job, car repossessed and my grandfather. I can imagine you saying I cannot get a break, right?

Things got so bad. I remember we cashed in my daughter's money from her penny bank to buy food. She was so happy. Little did she know that Mom was struggling. Pay attention to the small moments . My daughter was so happy you would have thought nothing was going on. I was good if she was happy. That is what mothers do, right?

That is how God work, that's joy.

The joy of the Lord is my strength. (Nehemiah 8:10)

One thing leads to another: brokenness, insecurity, betrayal, prosecution, just being fed up and tired of struggling. You know the saying when you are doing good, feel like you are getting ahead but something always come up. Seems like every time you take one step forward and then two steps backwards.

See? I put my hand in God's hands. Sure, everything in me wanted to give up, but something in me said, "Keep going." That something is the Holy Spirit.

My hand may not be your hand, but we all are dealt with one—that's life. Trails and tribulations come not only to make us stronger but to bring us closer to our father our lord and Savior Jesus Christ. Each day as you set aside devoting your time to the lord it will deepen and awakening your spirit to see God in way like you have never seen. It is not about RELIGION it is all about RELATIONSHIP.

Remember God loves you and so do I.

"I and my Father are one." — John 10:30

"I have told you these things, so that in me you may have peace. In this world you will have trouble. But take heart! I have overcome the world." —John 16:33

What is in your hand?

Write them here: _____

Today I, (insert your name), give you, Lord, my hand, my worries, my fears, everything from my past and any adversity that I may face now or what is still yet to come I trust you and I know that I am not alone in Jesus's name.

I believe in you, sis it your time! Get closer

Remember, God loves you, and so do I.

Today's Truth: First Things First

If you openly declare
that Jesus is Lord and
believe in your heart
that God raised him
from the dead, you will
be saved.

Romans 10:9

Open your mouth. Say it: "Jesus is my Lord." Connect it with your heart. You cannot feel saved. You must believe it with your whole heart. No matter what happens in life, who comes or goes, or what you do, you are saved. Know that Jesus is your ruler, of everything, this whole entire world, and he has all power in his hands.

God loves you and so do I.

Today's Truth: Goodbye but Not Forever

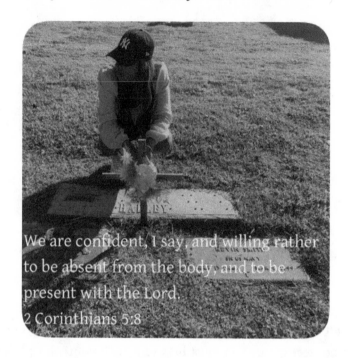

We are confident, I say, and willing rather to be absent from the body, and to be present with the Lord.
2 Corinthians 5:8

Losing a loved one can be very hard. Especially when it is unexpected. You try to hold on to the memories of the good times. Oftentimes you may question God, why? Thinking to yourself of what-ifs.

None of us will be here forever, but as believers, we can hold to God's promises knowing that we will see our loved ones on the other side. They are with Jesus and safe. Be encouraged today to smile because goodbye doesn't mean forever.

Remember, God loves you and so do I.

Today's Truth: You Are Equipped for It

FOR GOD GAVE US A SPIRIT
NOT OF FEAR
BUT OF POWER AND
LOVE AND
SELF-CONTROL.

2 TIMOTHY 1:7

There are many things in life that can bring fear. For example, losing a loved one, not knowing how you're going to pay your bills, sickness, crime, toxicity, addiction, relocation, parenting, marriage, or it can be just starting a new career or that new business with little or no support.

Truth is, fear will come, but remember it didn't come from God. So you don't have to give into it. You must keep going. The Holy Spirit that works on the inside of you will give you power, the love and self-control to move in faith instead of staying in fear.

Remember, God loves you and so do I.

Today's Truth: Get Up

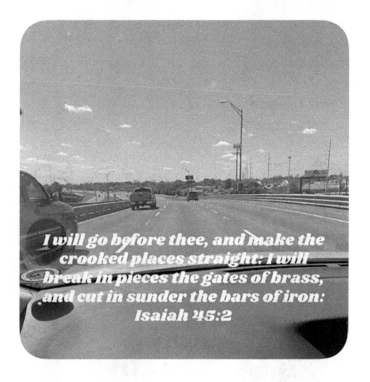

I will go before thee, and make the crooked places straight: I will break in pieces the gates of brass, and cut in sunder the bars of iron:
Isaiah 45:2

God put before us the Word. *Before* means he's in front of us. In life, you will fall, but it's never how you fall; it's how you get back up. You may be dealing with a fall in your life, whether it's divorce, parenting, finances, abuse, addiction, depression, or job loss. Truth is we all will fall at some point, but don't let the enemy trick you into staying there. Get up! You are not alone. God loves you and has you in the palm of his hands. You are safe and secure. Your dreams will not die. It's not the end; it's only a chapter, the story is still being written. Keep dreaming, keep believing.

Remember, God loves you and so do I.

Today's Truth: The Power of the Unseen

No matter what you face or what state of mind you find yourself in, the truth is, you won't stay there. The miracle first starts in your mind before it manifests into the physical first. Remember, God's ways are not your ways. Stand on God's Word. If he said it, believe no matter what you face. Our homes, jobs, businesses, friendships, and clothes are all temporary—but God is forever. Smile today; your coming out bigger and better.

Remember, God loves you and so do I.

Today's Truth: Call Him

One of the greatest tricks of the enemy is to get you to shut Up (stop worshipping) because of what you did or who you are. Remember these five letters: J, E, S, U, S.

When you don't understand...

When you can't pay your bills...

When betrayal hits...

When divorce comes...

When your single...

When you are parenting…

When you are broken…

When you are alone…

When you are misunderstood…

When you need a friend…

When your body is wrapped with pain

Stop calling people and call to Jesus. It's time. Wake up your inner man.

Remember, God loves you and so do I.

Today's Truth: It's Bigger than you.

A discipline means a follower of Jesus Christ. Our job is to love not only ourselves but everyone, even the ones that hate you, slander your name or even betrayed you. I remember one time on the job I would experience so much prosecution because of my belief or because I refuse to bite into negativity try to find good in any situation. I was literally being myself but no matter what I did they would always find something to pick on me about. It went far as me losing my job. Sure, I wanted to go off, I was hurt. I'm always reminded that I represent someone and that is bigger than me. So, I challenge you today to show love despite. Love from a distance if you have too.

Remember God loves you and so do I.

Today's Truth: Sweet Grace.

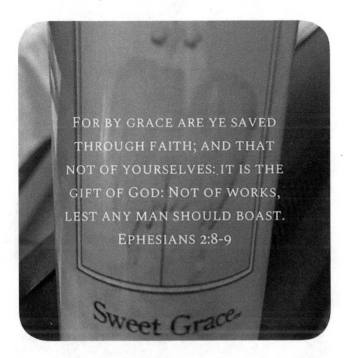

FOR BY GRACE ARE YE SAVED THROUGH FAITH; AND THAT NOT OF YOURSELVES: IT IS THE GIFT OF GOD: NOT OF WORKS, LEST ANY MAN SHOULD BOAST.
EPHESIANS 2:8-9

Sweet Grace

You ever gone to an ATM machine and try to make a transaction to withdraw money, but you didn't have enough or no money to complete transaction, and you get a receipt says *insufficient funds?* Well, in this case, God is your bank and Grace is the money and what makes it so amazing is that it never runs out. It's sufficient; not insufficient. You cannot earn it. That's what make it so sweet. Take a deep breathe, inhale and exhale.

Remember, God loves you and so do I.

Today's Truth : Look up for Strength

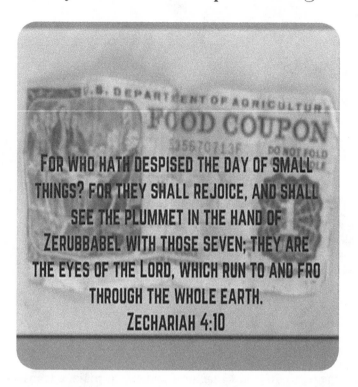

FOR WHO HATH DESPISED THE DAY OF SMALL THINGS? FOR THEY SHALL REJOICE, AND SHALL SEE THE PLUMMET IN THE HAND OF ZERUBBABEL WITH THOSE SEVEN; THEY ARE THE EYES OF THE LORD, WHICH RUN TO AND FRO THROUGH THE WHOLE EARTH.
ZECHARIAH 4:10

You must embrace where you are at today, right now. If God allowed it, he'll give you the strength to get through it. Instead of complaining or being down, look back at the times God brought you from. Things could be worse. You may not be where you want to be but thank God you are not where you used to be. Never ever give up.

Remember, God loves you and so do I.

Tuesday Truth: Gods Plan

Oftentimes, we have plans for our lives and some come through and some don't. Not because we did something wrong, but because God had a better plan for our lives, so this year 2020, I encourage you to let the Holy Spirit and God order every step you take. Say yes to his will and his ways, let us have a strong year.

Remember, God loves you and so do I.

page 5 of devotional

Today's Truth: Godfidence

I AM CERTAIN
THAT GOD
WHO BEGAN
THE GOOD WORK
within you, will continue
·H I S· ◆WORK◆ UNTIL
IT IS FINALLY
FINISHED

PHILIPPIANS 1:6

Godfidence is trusting in God, not ourselves.

When we are faced with disappointments, grief, betrayal, abuse both physical and mental, sickness, addiction, unemployment, divorce, anxiety, or depression—whatever your issue is that allows you to feel less than—be encouraged today. Hold on to your faith. Keep fighting and know that whatever he started, he will surely finish, no matter what comes your way.

Today's Truth: No Greater Love

In life, we are faced with circumstances that leave us feeling unloved. Things like divorce, relationships, sickness, rebellious children, abandonment, unemployment, single parenting, or the loss of a loved one. Whatever it is, remember that no matter what you face today or in the future, you are a child of the highest and he takes cares of his children. There is no love greater than God's love.

Remember, God loves you and so do I.

Today's Truth: Make Room for the New

EVERY BRANCH IN ME THAT
DOES NOT PRODUCE FRUIT HE REMOVES,
AND HE PRUNES EVERY BRANCH THAT
PRODUCES FRUIT SO THAT IT WILL
PRODUCE MORE FRUIT.

JOHN 15:2

Think about that old fruit you have in the refrigerator. It's rotten, all black, you can't eat it. Why? Because it's bad for you, right? God is saying to you that he will take out the bad fruit which is guilt, hatred, jealousy, unforgiveness, selfishness, anger, frustration, and he will give us love, joy, peace, patience, gentleness, kindness, self-control, faithfulness, and longsuffering. These are the good fruits of the Spirit that we as believers are to walk in every day. No, it will not be easy, but remember you are representing Jesus, not your will but his.

Remember, God loves you and so do I.

Today's Truth: Safe Place

The word *shall* mean *will*. In other words, what the Word of God says— if you look for me not with half, not a piece, but with *all* your heart—I *will* be there. Oftentimes we open our hearts up to the wrong things and people, which leads to brokenness or hurt, but today is a new day. Instead of telling someone what's in your heart, sit still and tell Jesus he's waiting and remember it's safe place.

Remember, God loves you and so do I.

Today's Truth: Believe It or Not, It is Working for Your Good

In this life, you will encounter trouble you cannot go around. The devil will hit you hard, especially being a child of God. But no matter how hard or bad things get in your life, just know it is working for your good. What does not kill you makes you stronger.

Remember, God loves you and so do I.

Today's Truth: Let Your Light Shine

In your darkest hours, your light still shines because Jesus lives in you. When people see you, they are supposed to see Jesus, his characteristics: love, joy, kindness, humility, respect, and integrity. Someone needs your light today, let it shine.

Remember, God loves you and so do I.

Today's Truth: Return to Sender

Every thought or imagination that comes to your mind today that says you're not good enough, you're not strong enough, you're not smart enough for the position, you will never make it, you'll never overcome those painful moments of your past, you'll never be delivered from addiction, God doesn't love you, or things won't get any better for you, guess what, the devil is a lie. You have the power to take hold and speak to that thing "RTS" (return to sender) back to pits of hell where it came from. You are not a victim; you are a victor. Take back your power. It starts in your mind.

Remember, God loves you and so do I.

Today's Truth: You Can Bury the Burden, but You Can't Carry the Load

COME TO ME, ALL YOU WHO ARE WEARY AND BURDENED, AND I WILL GIVE YOU REST.

MATTHEW 11:28

As women, we have so many responsibilities and carry so much weight. We were taught to be strong every day and ignore the pain or issues that we hold in our hearts, the ones that no one can see. We must allow those emotions and feelings to come up and out. It was not until I stopped going to people, instead I turned to Jesus to cry out. Then my healing started taking place from the inside.

Jesus will give you rest. The kind of rest that you can sleep well at night, when you're troubled on every side.

We can hide from others, but we cannot hide from Jesus.

Remember, God loves you and so do I.

Today's Truth: You Are Never Alone

Oftentimes, we fall under big stress when we hit the hardest times. The truth is, money isn't going to keep or make us happy. Things happen every day, but when you know that God will never fail or leave you, when you struggle to make ends meet, you can be content and have peace that you can't buy. In the good, the bad, and the ugly, God is with you.

Remember, God loves you and so do I.

Today's Truth: Trust God in the process

But forget not this one
thing, beloved, that one day
is with the Lord as a
thousand years, and a
thousand years as one day.
2 Peter 3:8

Do not let your feelings shift you or move you into something too soon that God is preparing you for.

Whatever you're in now, embrace it. The key is to master the day—your now, not next month or tomorrow but today. Time is limitless to God.

Remember, God loves you and so do I.

Today's Truth: Pray about Everything, Worry about Nothing

Starting all over, whether it's leaving a spouse, single parenting, moving to a new neighborhood, starting a new career/job, getting out of your comfort zone, staring the business, bills, sickness, or you maybe you lost your job. Don't worry another second. Why? Because when life disappointments us—and it will—things happen. Romans 8:31 says, "If God be for us, then who can be against us?" Whatever or has happened, that can't stop you. The only way that can happen is if you talk to him just like you would talk to a friend or parent (pray). Every time you are anxious or confused, you immediately give it to God.

Pray, believe, receive.

Remember, God loves you and so do I.

Today's Truth: Let the Word Guide You

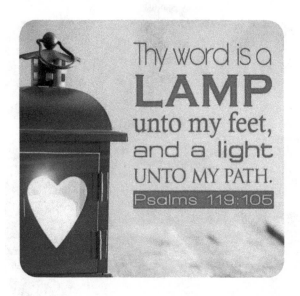

You ever try to walk in a dark room with no light? Bumping into everything, it's impossible for you to see, right? See, when we travel down dark roads in life and seek advice from a friend, loved one, companion, counselor, pastor, or maybe your own…nothing's wrong with that. But only the Word of God can lead us and guide out of every and any dark area in our lives. Don't waste another second driven by darkness. Stand on the Word, God, he will see you through. It's time for you to shine again.

Remember, God loves you and so do I.

Today's Truth: Live from Within

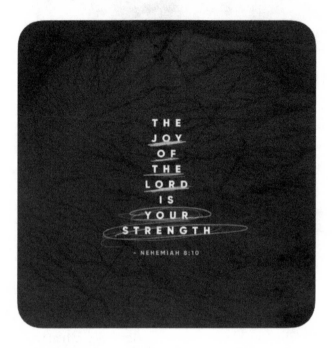

Having nice clothes, shoes, bags, a fancy car, a house, a job, marriage, a degree, a successful business—you living your best life, right? Ask yourself, if all of the material things are gone, if my husband leaves, friends run out, family turn their back, or I go through a season like Job and lose everything, could you still be happy?

What makes you is what's on the inside? How happy you get when you do the little things like give the homeless person on the side a dollar or food. It's something on the inside that makes you stronger, even while you go through your own issues and challenges. Feed into it because that's the joy, the Lord. He's saying, "Look at my child, with whom I am well pleased." The world will give you many reasons to cry but... God gives you a lifetime of smiles. It comes from within.

Remember, God loves you and so do I.

Today's Truth: Up Your Trust Level

Thou wilt keep him in perfect peace, whose mind is stayed on thee: because he trusteth in thee.
Isaiah 26:3

God doesn't give us the peace like the world does. Meaning, when things are going good for you in your family, finances, and your personal life, that is the world at peace. God's peace is not defined by a feeling but it's understood simply by trusting His word. If you are not at peace today just up your trust level not in yourself but in God.

Remember, God loves you and so do I.

Today's Truth: It's a Two-Way Street

ONE
FRIEND
SHARPENS
ANOTHER.
PROVERBS 27:17

Today look around, evaluate your circle, the people in your life. Do they bring out the best in you or the worst in you? Don't just hold on to the years. Never value the length of the relationship over the strength of the relationship. Don't go around being the one who's doing the pouring and not receiving; that's with friends or a companion. Make sure your glass is full.

Stop going where you are tolerated.

Start going where you are celebrated.

Let go, even if it's you and Jesus right now. The right relationships come when you let go off the trash.

Remember, God loves you and so do I.

Today's Truth: You Get What You Give

Ever helped someone and you know they don't deserve it? That's mercy. It's being kind, showing forgiveness, compassion in spite of what he or she deserves. It doesn't always feel good, the thought of you being a fool for that someone. People may say, "You are being stupid, I would've did this or that..." Well, guess what, you are not; you are blessed. God gives us mercy every day we don't deserve, because he loves us and cares. Keep doing good out of the kindness of your heart. What you give, God will give it back to you.

Remember, God loves you and so do I.

In life, fear creep into the unknown—the new job, career, loss of a loved one financial difficulties, crime, sickness, racism, politics, or parenting. Whiteboard, it is will not take you out. Why? Because God is with you in the good, the bad, and the ugly.

Remember, God loves you and so do I..

Today's Truth: Wisdom Is Key

IF YOU NEED WISDOM, ASK OUR GENEROUS GOD, AND HE WILL **GIVE IT TO YOU.**

JAMES 1:5

To get wisdom is to get understanding. You must ask God for it. Ever had a situation or encounter and you felt like you knew what to do or weren't sure? You needed a little more clarity on what to do. It's simple, just take a deep breath and ask the Lord to give you wisdom in that matter. Wait on the Holy Spirit to give you an answer, but remember delay is not denial. We need God's wisdom to help us make the right choices. Don't try to do it on your own. It's time to let God help you.

Remember, God loves you and so do I.

Today's Truth: There's a Way Out

EACH PERSON IS TEMPTED WHEN THEY
ARE DRAGGED AWAY BY THEIR OWN
EVIL DESIRE AND ENTICED.

JAMES 1:14

This scripture encourages us to be aware when we are tempted. Ever felt like doing something or you did something that you know wasn't right? Like for example, going to bed angry with your loved one or your child for way too long, curse that driver out at the red light or the cashier who's rude at the checkout counter, stole something, put yourself in a relationship that God didn't assign for you, hang out with people or go to places that are ungodly or whatever it may be that thing that you say, "Ummm, this don't feel right." And you know God wouldn't be please with you. *Red flag:* That's temptation, and it's not God. As it is written in the Lord's Prayer: *"Lord, lead us not into temptation."*

Although God doesn't tempt us, when we fall into temptation—and we will because the flesh is weak—God will always provide a way out. But you must learn from it and practice every day not to do it again.

Remember, God loves you and so do I.

Today's Truth: One Day at a Time

SO DON'T WORRY ABOUT TOMORROW, FOR TOMORROW WILL BRING ITS OWN WORRIES.

MATTHEW 6:34

We often think about what's going to happen or the next step. For instance, it could be a health problem, figuring out a way to pay the bills, what you are going to eat next, what you going to wear, what's going to happen on the job or your children. Whatever your tomorrow may be, know that you are not in control. Let God do his job; he holds your tomorrow. Make do with what you have today and let God take care of the rest. Be encouraged today, one day at a time.

Remember, God loves you and so do I.

Today's Truth: Dare to be Different

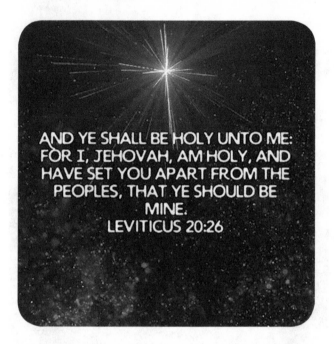

AND YE SHALL BE HOLY UNTO ME:
FOR I, JEHOVAH, AM HOLY, AND
HAVE SET YOU APART FROM THE
PEOPLES, THAT YE SHOULD BE
MINE.
LEVITICUS 20:26

As a believer and follower of Jesus Christ, certain things like old habits or patterns of living and relationships come to an end by the power of the Holy Spirit that lives on the inside of you. Be encouraged today to stand up and be strong. Everyone's not going to like you or accept the change that's taking place on the inside, or may not understand, and that's okay because it's not for them too. Be encouraged knowing that you are in the world but not of the world.

Remember, God loves you and so do I.

Today's Truth: Do You Really Believe?

Whatever you ask in prayer,
believe that you have received it,
and it will be yours.
—Mark 11:24

Ever felt like God does not hear you when you pray? Have you been praying about a certain thing or situation for some time now and things are still the same? Maybe it's not the prayer; it's what you believe. Do you really believe that things are already better? Remember, God is not moved by how much or how good we pray; he's move by our beliefs. Be encouraged today to believe in spite of....

Remember, God loves you and so do I.

Today's Truth: Walk in Your Power

Pure hearts are when you do something for someone not expecting nothing in return; in others words, doing it out of the kindness of your heart. Watch you motives, your inner being when making moves. Being blessed does not only refer to material things—the big house, the million dollars you have, the fancy car, businesses, beautiful looks—all that is good, but when you have integrity, moral courage, and a Godly character, you're unstoppable. You may not be there right now, that's okay, but be encouraged to ask for help. Say, "Lord Jesus, come into my heart. Create in me a clean heart and renew a right spirit within me." Walk in your power, sis.

Remember, God loves you and so do I.

Today's Truth: Watch Your Mouth

*Death and life are in the power
of the tongue: and they that love
it shall eat the fruit thereof.
Proverbs 18:21*

The tongue is a powerful weapon. You can either speak life or death. Speak words of encouragement to yourself. We all have days when we are down and out. Truth of the matter is when we start to speak and tell ourselves the negative than it becomes or reality. Be encouraged today to watch your mouth grandma always said if you don't have nothing good to say don't say it at all. You may be at a crossroads with life right now, sure you can say a lot of bad, sad, things and you may be saying well I have nothing good to say right now. Three words Thank You Jesus even when you are going through because he will see you through. You have your life that is enough. Talk to yourself like someone you love.

Remember God loves you and so do I..

Today's Truth: There's No In-between

Today's scripture encourages us to not (command) love the world—meaning drugs, sex, fame, gambling, intoxication—you know, the material things: flesh, desire more than him. It's either you're going to love the world or love God, and to love God is to do his will. There is no in-between, and if you are a child of God, a born-again believer, it is virtually impossible for you to love or do those things that you used to do.

Although you will be tempted if and when that occurs, and there will always be an interruption in your spirit that stops you. Sure, you will lose friends or often be misunderstood by people you are close with. People will say things like, "Oh, you've change, or you're so holy now, huh?" Some even call me Sister Walker. Simply replay "There's no in-between." Walk it like you talk it.

Remember, God loves you and so do I.

Today's Truth: Born to Win

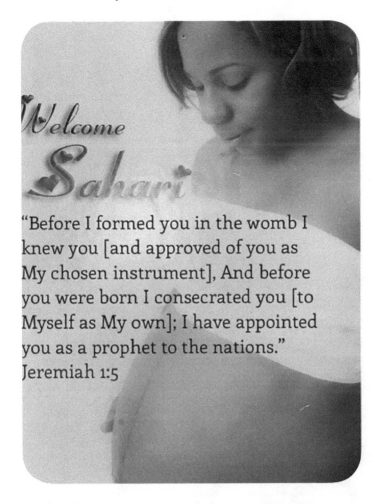

Welcome Sahari

"Before I formed you in the womb I knew you [and approved of you as My chosen instrument], And before you were born I consecrated you [to Myself as My own]; I have appointed you as a prophet to the nations." Jeremiah 1:5

You ever wonder why you are here on earth or ask the question, "What is my purpose?"

See, God knows you by name, and no matter what life throws your way, how many times you fall, you can and will always get back up because you were born to win. All you have to do is keep going, never ever give up on yourself. There is greatness inside of you. Believe it and receive it.

Remember, God loves you and so do I.